THE WORLD THROUGH GOD'S EYES

The World Through God's Eyes

Copyright © 2018 Chris Akatta-Okeke. All rights reserved.

No rights claimed for public domain material, all rights reserved. No parts of this publication may be reproduced, stored in any retrieval system, or transmitted in any form or by any means, electronic, mechanical, recording, or otherwise, without the prior written permission of the author. Violations may be subject to civil or criminal penalties.

ISBN: 978-1-63308-443-8 Paperback
       978-1-63308-444-5 Digital

Interior and Cover Design by *R'tor John D. Maghuyop*

1028 S Bishop Avenue, Dept. 178
Rolla, MO 65401

Printed in United States of America

THE WORLD THROUGH GOD'S EYES

WORLDLY REGIME VERSUS **GODLY REGIME**

CHRIS AKATTA-OKEKE

CHALFANT ECKERT
PUBLISHING

TABLE OF CONTENTS

Acknowledgement.. 7

Dedication... 9

About the Book.. 11

Chapter 1: Modern Society's Adverse Effects on Godliness........ 13

Chapter 2: Worldly Regime versus Godly Regime...................... 27

Chapter 3: God's Manual for Successful Family Relationships ... 47

Chapter 4: When a Man Loves a Woman................................... 69

Scripture Quotations.. 83

ACKNOWLEDGEMENT

I wish to extend my thanks to the Trinity for divine power, grace, knowledge, and His faithfulness. Through these, I was inspired and motivated to complete this project. My everlasting appreciation is to God Almighty, who granted me divine peace and harmony to compile this manuscript while facing the challenges of incarceration at HMP High Down.

Thank you, Jesus, I give you all the praise and honour.

I also want to acknowledge and thank my parents, Chief and Chief Mrs H. A Okeke (Omeifeukwu Mbaukwu) for their loving efforts to make me a good person.

DEDICATION

I dedicate this book to all practising Christians, those willing and obedient to the teachings of Christ Jesus, and to my brothers and sisters in Christ who taste and hunger for God. I also dedicate it to new converts whose desires are to follow the Scripture of truth and knowledge of our Saviour. And I would not want to forget my spiritual mentors, my wife and children, whose compassionate love and care brought me this far by the grace of God.

ABOUT THE BOOK

This book provides a pathway for struggling Christians (and society in general) who are persuaded by the prevailing social norms contrary to the doctrine and the Word of God for decent living.

By careful selection of Scriptures, the content of this documentary will give you the opportunity to discover how to live life out of this narrative, and how to respond wisely and biblically to the social and ethical challenges you face today. These teachings are designed both for mature Christians who may have gone astray and want to turn back to God's ways, and for younger Christians who need support for specific issues they face but lack the spiritual grounding to navigate the circumstances alone.

After reading this book, you will be able to evaluate your Christian walk and compare it to God's will for your life. It is my hope that these words will propel you to positively embrace the person and personality God created you to be, and help you to deepen your relationship with God, your family, friends and the Holy Spirit.

These pages contain life-changing extracts that will address worldly scepticism and rationalism tormenting society and relationships today, and give you weapons of spiritual warfare to conquer issues that plague your peace.

I pray you find the content of this book interesting, and that it addresses your needs accordingly to the glory of God. Enjoy it, relate to it personally and use it for group study.

Thank you and God bless!

Chris Akatta-Okeke

CHAPTER 1

MODERN SOCIETY'S ADVERSE EFFECTS ON GODLINESS

Mankind has evolved through many civilisation models, and each has not been without challenges. As civilizations have progressed, so have incidents of abnormality. The people of Sodom and Gomorrah plunged so deeply into dysfunction that it became the norm and was accepted. The same thing has happened in societies since then, and our modern cultures are no different and no better. We tend to misplace our priorities, misuse our power, and operate from wrong motives. 2 Timothy 3:1 – 5 (NIV) tells us

> *…There will be terrible times in the last days. People will be lovers of themselves, lovers of money, boastful, proud, abusive, disobedient to their parents, ungrateful, unholy, without love, unforgiving, slanderous, without self-control, brutal, not lovers of the good, treacherous, rash, conceited, lovers of pleasure rather than lovers of God—having a form of godliness but denying its power. Have nothing to do with such people.*

MODERN SOCIETY'S ADVERSE EFFECTS ON GODLINESS

Many people have lost godliness by making personal choices that endorse ungodliness. Some demonstrate outward godly appearances but under the surface deny and blaspheme God's power. It has become socially acceptable to justify abominations and corrupt practices. We must not get caught up in immoral webs and we need to avoid unholy trends and remember that all that glitters is not gold.

Human beings think they are smart and they allow themselves to be swayed by unprofitable desires, socially acceptable but ungodly norms, vile teachings, and abominable practices. They go on quests for learning but are blind to the truth of God's Word.

Professing themselves to be wise, they became fools
Romans 1:22 (KJV)

*There is a way which seemeth right unto a man,
but the end thereof are the ways of death.*
Proverbs 4:12 (KJV)

You are no doubt aware of the escalating crime rate and the breakdown of law and order. No matter how many new laws are enacted, the crime rate continues to surge, making more work for the already overwhelmed judiciary. Despite tougher penalties and imposed sanctions, the crime rate is still on the rise. A prudent person would contemplate why this is occurring. With most countries in the European economic areas and many other countries around the world toughening punishments associated to crimes, why aren't criminal deterred? What makes them re-offend? Where do they get the desire to break the law while knowing the punishment will be severe? There must be fundamental reasons why the judiciary and government agencies have not derived the expected good results of reduced recidivism.

Part of the reason for continued criminal offence is that parental wisdom and instruction (much of it derived from biblical principles) aren't being passed on with the same reverence and respect as they were in previous generations. Life lessons shared with the younger generation are shrugged off as obsolete, old-fashioned, outdated and awkward. Our parents' generation saw discipline as instructional but modern society sees it as abusive. Setting aside conventional and proven wisdom results in finding wrong answers to life's questions. Each successive generation seems to be getting further away from what worked in the past, and new problems continue to surface as a result.

When situations get out of hand, people seek to control them by either blaming the parents, the type of upbringing, or the role of the parents. The home suddenly becomes relevant. The rest of the time leading up to crisis and conflict is wrought with neglectful attitudes about the importance of parental roles and advice and the positive impact they can have on a child. The people who discredit the significance of effective parenting are the ones who criticise and accuse every good intention of a parent as being harsh, abusive, and sometimes uninformed and non-achievable in current social climate.

> *Hear, ye children, the instruction of a father, and attend to know understanding. For I give you good doctrine, forsake ye not my law. For I was my father's son, tender and only beloved in the sight of my mother. He taught me also, and said unto me, Let thine heart retain my words: keep my commandments, and live.*
> Proverbs 4:1-4 (KJV)

I heard something refreshing from a young motivational speaker and gained a measure of knowledge from what he said. Paraphrased here, he said, 'What your parents tell you and teach you about are mainly what they already know through their mistakes over the years or what they have witnessed from experience. Better still, what they fear not to happen to you as their children and loved ones.'

MODERN SOCIETY'S ADVERSE EFFECTS ON GODLINESS

The audience went quiet for a moment as they pondered the truth of this youth's statement. After all, wasn't he correct? What parent would want to be responsible for their child becoming a failure, a troubled child, or at risk of being either? What parent doesn't want the best for the children they brought into this world? What parent would deny their children correction when they offend or err?

The Scripture says

If a son shall ask bread of any of you that is a father,
will he give him a stone? or if he ask a fish,
will he for a fish give him a serpent?
Or if he shall ask an egg, will he offer him a scorpion?
If ye then, being evil, know how to give good gifts unto
your children: how much more shall your heavenly
Father give the Holy Spirit to them that ask him?
Luke 11:11-13 (KJV)

The things I write are inspired by the Holy Spirit. We must encourage one another with the Word of God as the learning and teaching manual for Christians and believers in our Lord and Saviour Jesus.

The escalated rate of offending and re-offending in this present age have come to stay, and will possibly increase because the man-made laws enacted in this present dispensation are corrupt and against the laws of God who is the Creator of all things.

Contrary to the knowledge and grace given freely through Jesus Christ, even those who ought to know what is proper have compromised the truth. Fearful of being challenged and chastised by a corrupt, phobic, and adulterous society, they refuse to speak the truth.

Train up a child in the way he should go:
and when he is old, he will not depart from it.
Proverbs 22:6 (KJV)

One day I was stationary in my taxi at the rank in Eyre Square, Galway, when a woman walked up to me and asked me, 'Did you see a camera at the back of your taxi car seat?'

I took a look at the back of my seat and answered, 'No.' Then I asked her, 'Why, what happened?'

She said her fifteen-year-old daughter was out partying the night before at the city centre and forgot her camera at the back seat of the taxi at about 3 a.m. on her way back to Oughterard, Co. Galway, about 40 kilometres from the city centre.

As I intended to assist, I asked this woman, 'What did your fifteen-year-old daughter come to do in town that late?'

The woman replied that her daughter came to meet with her boyfriend.

I told her that I will contact the person in our group in charge of handling lost and found complaints. I now further asked this woman 'Why is your daughter not with you to help find or identify the vehicle where she left the camera?'

She replied me saying that she did not want to push her daughter too much because she didn't want the daughter to report her to ISPCC (*Irish Society for the Prevention of Cruelty to Children*).

I was shocked! The mother of this girl was out looking for her own camera that the daughter misplaced and was afraid to bring the daughter along to help with the search because of what the daughter might say to ISPCC. This is but one of thousands of examples of the adverse influence of modern civilisation on our society.

> *Apply* thine *heart* unto *instruction,*
> *and thine ears to the words* of *knowledge.*
> *Withhold* not *correction* from the *child: for if thou*
> *beatest* him with the *rod,* he shall not *die.*
> Proverbs 23:12-13 (KJV)

MODERN SOCIETY'S ADVERSE EFFECTS ON GODLINESS

> *Now no chastening for the present seemeth to be joyous, but grievous: nevertheless afterward it yieldeth the peaceable fruit of righteousness unto them which are exercised thereby.*
> Hebrews 12:11 (KJV)

The woman searching for the missing camera knew that what her daughter had done was wrong and she didn't approve of it. However, she lacked the confidence to correct and chasten her daughter because of fear of being brought to disrepute. She chose to accommodate and accept her daughter's errors rather than face societal outrage. If her daughter continues in the way she is going, she will surely end up on the wrong path that could lead to dropping out of school, getting pregnant out of wedlock, taking drugs or abusing alcohol, being involved in public disorderliness and ultimately affecting her choices for the future.

Is it any wonder that juvenile delinquency is increasing at an alarming rate? Many parents have lost the grip of their God-given position and right as the parent and first teacher for their children. For some parents, government policies have simply stripped them of their rights to train, advise and nurture their children to make good choices. Parents blame the government, children blame their parents, and neither should play the blame game.

There is no legitimate excuse to renege on parental responsibilities. If a child goes astray, there are consequences for the child and the parent. If a child stays on the straight and narrow way led by involved godly parents, there are rewards for the child and the parent. Government policies mainly focus on provisions for the protection of vulnerable members of society, but unfortunately, it's not the primary duty of any government to nurture a child. No parent should allow themselves to be confused into thinking that the government knows best what is good for their children. Although sometimes challenging, parents and guardians still have the greatest impact and instil the best character in children. The government never will be able to do your job, only you can with God's help.

An upsurge in information technology occurred around the turn of the 21st century. Prior to the millennium (some of us remember it as Y2K), life was much simpler, had a slower pace, and learning took place by conventional methods. There was still respect, morality, and reservations. Societal norms were able to curb intent for wrongdoing, and families protected their values and members, and by doing so encouraged sound discretion in day-to-day decisions.

Once we became indoctrinated and embraced the electronic age, the internet and social media became part of our social fabric. The pace picked up and now learning and access to information is instant and at our fingertips. Awareness through access to information has improved our lives in many ways. However, it has by its development and expansion exposed our young people to nefarious concepts and has negatively influenced some individuals who lack self-control. In other words, anything goes! No reservations, no hesitation, and no one cares. With all the increased knowledge and advancement in science and technology, you would think the world would be a safer, better place to live. What has occurred instead is that mankind has chosen to follow paths which are worldly, corrupt beyond boundaries, lacking spiritual recipe and ethnic origin. In other words, we are far from God and in trouble.

> *The fear of the Lord is the beginning of wisdom:*
> *a good understanding have all they that do*
> *his commandments: his praise endureth for ever.*
> Psalm 111:10 (KJV)

> *The fear of the Lord is the beginning of knowledge:*
> *but fools despise wisdom and instruction.*
> Proverbs 1:7 (KJV)

MODERN SOCIETY'S ADVERSE EFFECTS ON GODLINESS

Praise ye the Lord. Blessed is the man that feareth the Lord, that delighteth greatly in his commandments. His seed shall be mighty upon earth: the generation of the upright shall be blessed. Wealth and riches shall be in his house: and his righteousness endureth for ever.
Psalm 112:1-3 (KJV)

On St. Patrick's Day (March 17th) a few years ago, I was at Victoria Place Corner in Eyre Square in Galway. I noticed a young boy I knew within the South African and Nigerian community. He was thirteen years old and boldly smoking in public walking down a side street with a female friend. I called to him and admonished him for smoking. He was too young to smoke and it was bad for his health. I was taken aback at his response. He informed me that I was not his father and he didn't have to listen to me.

On another occasion, I was driving home some female friends from a night out. They were Polish women and among them was a young black woman. Her speech was quite offensive and filled with frequent use of the *F* word. At some point in the four-mile journey, I had to speak out concerning my dislike for the way she spoke, and I tried to correct the perceived impression that it was trendy to speak in such manner. She got very rude to the extent that even her Polish friends had to calm her down. Her friends understood the points I made. I am a parent to adolescents of African origin and was disgusted by the vile and unpleasant words from this girl who was close to the same age as my daughters. I challenged her goths and her justification when she said it was none of my business how she chose to speak.

'No,' I said, 'because how you speak is not typical of a decent Nigerian family who have immigrated to Ireland to forge ahead with their family. I insisted she had to consider my advice and to change rather than rubbish it.

> *'Children, obey your parents in the Lord, for this is right.*
> *'Honor your father and mother' —which is the first*
> *commandment with a promise— 'so that it may go well*
> *with you and that you may enjoy long life on the earth.'*
> Ephesians 6:1-3 (NIV)

Members of parliaments and senators who legislate to enact civil liberty laws do not allow their children and wards to be negatively influenced by the contents of the laws. They still uphold the need to apply best practices towards a humble, decent behaviour for better living. As much as everyone has a right of choice, most elites and responsible parents still try their best to love and cultivate moral values into their family members.

Unfortunately, liberty of choices has led many down the wrong path of life, and has sometimes destroyed dreams, broken homes and brought all sort of sorrows to many.

> *"All things are lawful," but not all things are profitable;*
> *"All things are lawful," but not all edify.*
> 1 Corinthians 10:23 (Berean Literal Bible)

> *'Dress the way you want to be addressed.'*
> Bianca Frazier

The body is not meant for sexual immorality. It is the temple of God, so we ought to honour God with our bodies by dressing modestly and professionally. When a woman dresses inappropriately by exposing her body and curves in public, she deliberately attracts disrespectful, provocative comments. These vulgar comments are spoken because of her sexually provocative mode of dressing, and she becomes the architect of undignified invitations and lustful flirtations.

MODERN SOCIETY'S ADVERSE EFFECTS ON GODLINESS

Dress for success. That means dress suitably for the occasion. If you are going to work, dress for the job. Likewise, if you are out shopping or at the train station, dress appropriately. Half-naked night club garb will garner you no respect. When you go church, dress up and look nice. Ladies, if you don't want to be mocked and embarrassed by passers-by, cover up and dress suitably to reflect clean, decent upbringing and the morals your parents tried to teach you.

Don't expect the government (including the school system) to train your children in areas that you as a parent are responsible to teach. What the government is responsible for is promulgating laws against sexual harassment, targeted against individuals who stalk, and those who pass derogatory and sexually explicit remarks to ladies and other vulnerable persons. Everyone is responsible for their own actions, and there is no excuse for such remarks and actions. Having said that, these types of behaviours are on the rise but can be reduced by dressing appropriately.

There are lots of lessons to be learnt from home. One could cut a tree, but if the tree is not rooted out, it's likely to grow again. The same applies when people lack decent home training and discipline; they are likely to continue with challenges on issues that could be avoided.

> *Do you not know that your bodies are temples of the Holy Spirit, who is in you, whom you have received from God? You are not your own; you were bought at a price. Therefore honour God with your bodies.*
> 1 Corinthians 6:19-20 (NIV)

Public funds that should be invested in growing the economic sector are being diverted to social services. Why? Because of continued absence of discipline and lack of home training, the younger generation is costing national and local governments a fortune. Increased demand for social services is taking priority over other aspects of governance. Issues such as juvenile delinquency, child abuse, substance abuse, lack of motivation, depression and a myriad of other avoidable social issues of youth are sucking up the funds that should be used to run other government programs.

Frontline public servants are feeling the brunt of the youth crisis. Police, doctors, nurses, and social care service staffs, even taxi operators face daily challenges in dealing and managing members of the public. Deliberate misbehaviour is frequently linked to right to freedom and liberty stances.

Our frontline service workers are golden members of society. The saying that gold is meant for those who know its value is true. Police are spat at, called names and kicked while performing their duties. Many of the offenders never see the inside of a courtroom for their disrespectful acts because the courts are packed with more serious offenders. Health workers trying to save lives are being threatened and physically abused, while perpetrators are inconsiderate of the lifesaving assistance our doctors and nurses are rendering. Likewise, public service vehicle operators delivering essential taxi and transport services put up with threats, abuse, and the responsibility of babysitting even adult users. They constantly face name calling, derogatory remarks, racially-motivated actions, and sometimes are short paid for service provided. The situation has resulted in many frontline workers quitting their jobs to avoid the degenerating circumstances emerging from disruptive characters in today's society.

Government agencies are introducing new laws and devising cutting-edge security measures to safeguard the public. However, crime seems to rise to meet the new technologies and statutes and our society is afflicted by the acute symptom of disorderliness that likely stems from dilapidated values and inappropriate family orientation. Providing more resources certainly does help but might not provide a long-term solution. We need to address the causes along with the effects – the roots of the problems along with the symptoms and manifestations.

We have to be careful not to think we have become wiser than our Creator, God the Father. He created us in His image and He alone can help us out of our current societal dilemmas and problems. If we adhere to God's commandments and are obedient to what the Scriptures teach, the civilisation we crave is possible, human development and advancement will occur, and our society will not be vile.

SUBMISSION TO AUTHORITIES

Let everyone be subject to the governing authorities, for there is no authority except that which God has established. The authorities that exist have been established by God. Consequently, whoever rebels against the authority is rebelling against what God has instituted, and those who do so will bring judgment on themselves. For rulers hold no terror for those who do right, but for those who do wrong. Do you want to be free from fear of the one in authority? Then do what is right and you will be commended. For the one in authority is God's servant for your good. But if you do wrong, be afraid, for rulers do not bear the sword for no reason. They are God's servants, agents of wrath to bring punishment on the wrongdoer.
Romans 13:1-4 (NIV)

Though a sinner do evil an hundred times, and his days be prolonged, yet surely I know that it shall be well with them that fear God, which fear before him:
Ecclesiastes 8:12 (KJV)

But it shall not be well with the wicked, neither shall he prolong his days, which are as a shadow; because he feareth not before God.
Ecclesiastes 8:13 (KJV)

God bless you…

CHAPTER 2

WORLDLY REGIME VERSUS GODLY REGIME

Lifestyles change with the culture, and it is valid to question lifestyles as the cultural thinking adjusts. With those changes, often values and practices change and inadvertently infiltrate Christian choices. Believers in our Lord and Saviour Jesus Christ must pay attention to how cultural changes affect their Christian walk in terms of actions and beliefs that may run counter to Scripture.

As what is acceptable to society is modified, it becomes more difficult to advance and hold fast to basic character standards which define Christianity. It seems that decent people following scripturally sound lifestyle choices are almost obsolete in the world's eyes. Godly values communicated in modern society frequently create controversy.

Christian values are under attack making it hard to distinguish good from bad, virtuous from evil, truth from lies and validity from falsehood. Many people attribute the discord to changing times and the environment that ensues as a result. No matter the cause, a Christian has a lifelong commitment to the teaching and doctrine of Christ our Saviour and is responsible to uphold the faith.

Apostle Paul wrote –

WORLDLY REGIME VERSUS GODLY REGIME

> *What business is it of mine to judge those outside the church? Are you not to judge those inside?*
> 1 Corinthians 5:12 (NIV)

Christians face a peculiar plight when faced with the worldly regime. They face criticism and insult from friends, family, work colleagues and business associates who do not share their faith. It is grievous and impacts the depth of Christian practice. Many Christians are not steadfast in their confession and profession with Christ due to the flesh and societal mistreatment. Many avoid being known as *born again* Christians, while many fear being labelled by some influential personalities in their community. The power and pressure from these negative forces, coupled with fear of the unknown have compelled some Christians to compromise their faith rather than exercise it in the congregation of men and women.

I want to encourage you that Jesus knew all these things would happen, so He asked believers to stand firm, hold fast and not waver or be deceived. In the end, it will be worth it.

> *And because iniquity shall abound, the love of many shall wax cold. But he that shall endure unto the end, the same shall be saved.*
> Matthew 24:12-13 (KJV)

CHERRY PICKING CHRISTIANS

A friend uses a phrase I have come to understand and appreciate: *Cherry Picking Christians*. His definition encompasses people who say they are Christians but are not ready to adhere to the rules of being Christian. Neither are they concerned about the do's and don'ts of Christendom.

Even the game of soccer has rules and regulations to guide players, the coach and the clubs. If organized sports attract a following who know and expect players to follow the rules, should not the body of Christ know and be expected to follow the Commandments, biblical teachings, and counsel of our church leaders? When a physician gives us a prescription to get well, we take it. We rely on the doctor's wisdom in selecting the proper medical course of action to help us get well quickly. In the same manner, we can rely on the Great Physician, putting our trust and faith in Him who is still in the healing business. Thus, let us embrace Christian principles and biblical guidance so that it is well with us and with our souls.

When we as Christians sincerely follow the guiding Commandments of God, we will certainly derive good results, and have excellent outcome which further strengthens our faith, and allows us through example and good report to win more souls into the Kingdom.

Jesus said

> *If ye love me, keep my commandments.*
> *And I will pray the Father, and he shall give you another*
> *Comforter, that he may abide with you for ever;*
> John 14: 15-16 (KJV)

Church leaders have remarked frequently that a large proportion of new Christian converts are attracted to the promises of Jesus Christ and what He can do for them. Few are interested in what they can do for Christ; they want the blessings without the responsibilities. It takes a while, sometimes years, to learn that they cannot pick and choose what they want and interpret Scriptures to coincide and shore up their worldly circumstances. It takes maturation to realize that we do not fit Jesus into our lives but rather fit our lives around Him.

> *"All this I have spoken while still with you. But the Advocate, the Holy Spirit, whom the Father will send in my name, will teach you all things and will remind you of everything I have said to you.*
> John 14: 25-26 (NIV)

We must be *doers* of the Word, not just hearers, and we must guard our hearts so that we do not let the worldly regime dominate the truth. Churches are filled with people who claim to be Christians but do not live as Christians.

> *Not everyone who says to me, 'Lord, Lord,' will enter the kingdom of heaven, but only the one who does the will of my Father who is in heaven.*
> Matthew 7:21 (NIV)

CHALLENGES

Do you ever dwell on what you gave up in order to be a Christian? If so, you will become distracted. This sometimes happens to new Christians but can beset older people of faith as well. Instead of looking back at what you gave up, look back at what God gave up so that you could have salvation and what Jesus gave up to atone for your sins once and for all.

For God so loved the world, that he gave his only begotten son, that whosoever believeth in him should not perish, but have everlasting life.
John 3:16 (KJV)

The price to follow Christ is small compared to the benefits. Forget the cost, leave the past behind and make up your mind to follow Him. The Holy Spirit will guide, comfort and help you along the way. You can place your hope and trust in Christ. All things are possible with God.

…What is impossible with men is possible with God
Luke 18:27 (NIV)

BLACKMAIL

Be careful what you teach and what messages you send. Threatening, intimidation, extortion and other vices cause significant damage to the body of Christ. Negative worldly influences can corrupt and pollute the reputations of faithful Christians who normally co-exist in harmony with their brethren. Satan would like nothing better than to have God's people manipulate, blackmail and introduce human greed into the church, but this is not permissible in God's Kingdom, so be alert to the worldly factors you allow to influence you.

> *If anyone teaches otherwise and does not agree to the sound instruction of our Lord Jesus Christ and to godly teaching, they are conceited and understand nothing. They have an unhealthy interest in controversies and quarrels about words that result in envy, strife, malicious talk, evil suspicions and constant friction between people of corrupt mind, who have been robbed of the truth and who think that godliness is a means to financial gain. But godliness with contentment is great gain. For we brought nothing into the world, and we can take nothing out of it.*
> 1 Timothy 6:3-7 (NIV)

Be careful! Avoid controversy that could lead to blackmail, evil agendas and negative influences that are counter to or endanger God's will for His people.

Similarly, Proverbs tells us that

> *Pride goeth before destruction,
> and an haughty spirit before a fall.*
> Proverbs 16:18 (KJV)

Thinking too highly of ourselves based on worldly measures is dangerous in the Kingdom. When we consider ourselves above others based on possessions, education or other worldly standards of success and prestige, we get greedy and forget the grace God has given us. It doesn't take long until wickedness sets in. Instead, we must remember that all the good things in our lives came from God and we must remain sober and realistic in our self-assessment and appreciate our blessings. In a similar vein, children of God must do what is ethically in line with godliness, and with all purity of heart. If there be vengeance, let God apportion it; not us. We are to live life thoroughly saved and called to freedom in the Lord.

> *You, my brothers and sisters, were called to be free.*
> *But do not use your freedom to indulge the flesh;*
> *rather, serve one another humbly in love.*
> Galatians 5:13 (NIV)

FAMILY IS BEDROCK TO GOOD SOCIETY

A well cultivated and nurtured family system has always been, and will always be the bedrock of a thriving, sustaining and productive society and economy.

If we fail to address declining family values, our next generation will be in trouble. Family members have great influence over individuals and it is at the family level that the greatest change for good can occur. Values, good or bad, are passed on to children, and good parenting is vital to children's futures. When family values are constructive and positive, a child's future is much improved over the alternative. Parents present in the home enhance positive child development when compared to homes in which a parent is absent.

Wouldn't it be great if parents had training to be good parents? If there was a place they could go for encouragement, mentoring, and training? A place to teach them how to nurture children instead of abuse them physically and emotionally?

Social workers and other professionals have their hands full trying to protect families and children. Government statutes and laws have increased protections for our vulnerable citizens. Unfortunately, all the human efforts and expenses to improve family life do not target the root causes of the issues. We doctor the symptoms and the bandages we place on fundamental family issues can be seen everywhere. New symptoms emerge and instead of eradicating the root cause, we treat the symptoms.

How do we get back to basics of exemplary best practices in the home? What do I mean by that? A man provides for his family; the woman joins forces with him to provide for and protect the home; children are cared for until they can care for themselves. Children are raised in the fear and admonition of the Lord, educated, fed, clothed and provided shelter so that they have what is needed for essential living. Children are exposed to appropriate social systems, educational opportunities, sporting activities, Church, extended family circles and other facilities to enhance their variety of choices. Children must be trained to understand spiritual values and benefits of the family's denomination. Parents are a child's first earthly teachers, and God holds parents accountable for this significant life assignment.

Even animals protect and provide for their offspring. Like humans, it is written into their DNA. Effective childrearing is an important moral component of society. The types of society we have, and neighbourhoods we live in and the safety of our streets is determined in large measure by the upbringing afforded to the people who live there. Whether we respect one another and are law-abiding and productive, or whether we are troubled, disorderly and calamitous can be traced back to our upbringing.

What if a parent refuses to raise a child with a strong moral compass? What if they abandon their duties? We can expect violence, crime, disputes, abuse and lack of law and order to ensue. What a shame that the government and social workers must step in and take action because parents won't. They must investigate whether there is alcohol misuse, drug abuse, mental illness or bad habit responsible for the situation. In such instance, parents may lose custody, are referred for treatment, and sometimes prosecuted for criminal neglect or abuse. As a society, we need a strict benchmark and proper assessment before disenfranchising a parent's rights over their children.

There is still an immense need to encourage the traditional marriage system or the conventional marriage pattern, whereby a man and woman agree to join in holy matrimony to become husband and wife. This fundamental marriage method was ordained by God and is the only marriage in the Bible. Modern variations of the husband and wife bond for life are just that: modern variations, unscriptural, and not healthy to the soul or society. Media is full of attempts to promote and allow freedom of choice and to undermine traditional marriage between a man and woman. Christians must beware not to be sucked into this antithesis.

Procreation is a core reason for marriages. Fortunately, in a traditional marriage, this can be achieved biologically. Although vast scientific experimentation and innovations have assisted those who have difficulty conceiving, artificial methods have not replaced the quality and authenticity of babies born through natural means.

As Christians, we must be careful not to buckle to the pressure of the worldly regime. We must be ever vigilant to our beliefs about marriage by biblical principles between a man and a woman.

> *And be not conformed to this world: but be ye transformed by the renewing of your mind, that ye may prove what is that good, and acceptable, and perfect, will of God.*
> Romans 12:2 (KJV)

DEFEATING DOMESTIC CHALLENGES

Relationships face many challenges including domestic violence and sexism. Domestic violence is cruel, obnoxious and obscene. It is unacceptable and intolerable in any shape or form against anyone regardless of gender. Perpetrators devise acts of physical abuse or psychological torture to punish, intimidate and subdue their victims. Those acts are damaging to family union and relationships; their revolving effects tamper with the state of mind of the victims, including others who reside where such acts take place. When children are involved, their self-esteem, confidence and productivity at school and in the community are negatively impacted whether they are being abused or someone at home is the target. Therefore, issues of this nature should be carefully addressed.

We don't know the full impact of abuse, and we need to study the potential outcomes of long- and short-term abuse in troubled relationships and family structures. Anxiety, depression, fear, hatred, unforgiveness, revenge and many more emotions are most likely to surface and cause negative actions.

When Jesus walked the earth, His disciples asked Him which the greatest commandment was.

> *Jesus said unto him, Thou shalt love the Lord thy God with all thy heart, and with all thy soul, and with all thy mind. This is the first and great commandment. And the second is like unto it, Thou shalt love thy neighbour as thyself.*
> Matthew 22: 37-39 (KJV)

The application of these Scriptures to our daily living will encourage us to experience daily renewal of heart. In as much as we confess to love God, we must also love one another and withdraw from violence, quarrel, fights and abuse.

> *Then came Peter to him, and said, Lord,*
> *how oft shall my brother sin against me,*
> *and I forgive him? till seven times?*
> *Jesus saith unto him, I say not unto thee,*
> *Until seven times: but, Until seventy times seven.*
> Matthew 18: 21-22 (KJV)

God first showed us His love through the sacrifice of His only begotten son, Jesus. He taught us to emulate His example and forgive one another. There is no justification for hatred.

> *No one has ever seen God; but if we love one another,*
> *God lives in us and his love is made complete in us.*
> 1 John 4:12 (NIV)

God also forgave us of our sins. No matter how tough it may be, we must find it in our hearts to forgive others. If we are in Christ, forgiveness is infinite, we should always forgive. When Jesus taught the disciples to pray, forgiveness was in the essence of His teaching.

> *For if ye forgive men their trespasses,*
> *your heavenly Father will also forgive you:*
> Matthew 6:14 (KJV)

The worldly regime prefers to expound *an eye for an eye* approach, but as a Christian we advocate forgiveness and leave vengeance to the Lord. When we seek revenge, we allow Satan to rule over us. Though sometimes tough, Scripture encourages us to live in peace.

> *Do not take revenge, my dear friends, but leave room for God's wrath, for it is written: 'It is mine to avenge; I will repay,' says the Lord.*
> Romans 12:19 (NIV)

No matter the reason for quarrel or misunderstanding, Christians must opt for better and harmless ways of solving their issues. One of the best way is to call one of the wise among the church to assist in resolving the matter. Whatever the circumstance, the believer must not go before a forum of unbelievers to seek a solution to the matter. The Bible speaks plainly about the worldly regime not judging the Lord's people.

> *If any of you has a dispute with another, do you dare to take it before the ungodly for judgment instead of before the Lord's people? Or do you not know that the Lord's people will judge the world? And if you are to judge the world, are you not competent to judge trivial cases? Do you not know that we will judge angels? How much more the things of this life! Therefore, if you have disputes about such matters, do you ask for a ruling from those whose way of life is scorned in the church? I say this to shame you. Is it possible that there is nobody among you wise enough to judge a dispute between believers? But instead, one brother takes another to court—and this in front of unbelievers! The very fact that you have lawsuits among you means you have been completely defeated already. Why not rather be wronged? Why not rather be cheated? Instead, you yourselves cheat and do wrong, and you do this to your brothers and sisters. Or do you not know that wrongdoers will not inherit the kingdom of God? Do not be deceived: Neither the sexually immoral nor idolaters nor adulterers nor men who have sex*

> *with men nor thieves nor the greedy nor drunkards nor slanderers nor swindlers will inherit the kingdom of God. And that is what some of you were. But you were washed, you were sanctified, you were justified in the name of the Lord Jesus Christ and by the Spirit of our God.*
> 1 Corinthians 6:1-11 (NIV)

It is only by the grace of God that we are all saved, washed, sanctified and justified.

There is none righteous among us except for the righteousness of Christ. The difference between us and the world is that we are saved by grace in the name of our Lord Jesus.

As it is written:

> *"There is no one righteous, not even one;*
> Romans 3:10 (NIV)

Luckily, we can plead the blood of Jesus and ask Him to save us from worldly vices and propel us to understanding and intervention through His divine grace, mercy and favour.

SEXISM

In the past decade, gender equality has thrived and brought inclusion and diversity to communities, education, politics, the economy and other areas of influence. Unfortunately, before this enlightenment, women were marginalised, denied, and undervalued as integral parts of the economy and society. The inspiring pursuit of some notable women has brought about the much-needed change and inclusion: Maya Angelo, Margret Thatcher, Hillary Clinton, Opera Winfrey, Joyce Meyer and many more have campaigned or otherwise portrayed the much-needed recognition through their success and dynamism.

During the early fight for gender rights and equality, feminist groups crusaded and lobbied on important issues such as the right to vote, the right to equal employment opportunities and right to public speaking. As these rights were successfully accomplished and recognised, women continued to petition legislators and parliaments to grant rights to equality in the workplace, equal pay for equal work, and career advancement opportunities among others. As a result of their foremothers, today's women are CEOs, public administrators, and many countries have female prime ministers. Women participate in sporting events that were traditionally male in yesteryear: boxing, football, wrestling, etc. I genuinely applaud the immense achievement in the campaign led by feminist activists. Women's status in society has escalated to where it should have been long ago.

Women are now somebodies instead of nobodies, and their perceived intrinsic value has increased exponentially as God planned it from the beginning. However, the Bible does give distinct gender roles to both men and women regarding their place in families and societies.

The role of men is similar around the world: a man is male, a brother, a husband, a father, a provider, strong, loving and the head of his household. Likewise, a woman is female, a sister, a wife, a helpmate, a supporter, tender, loving and a homemaker.

WORLDLY REGIME VERSUS GODLY REGIME

The worldly regime is heading toward gender-free societies, but God intended men to be men and women to be women so that they would naturally perform best in their God-given roles. The world has compromised God's edicts and reasons for human existence.

> *So God created man in his own image,*
> *in the image of God created he him; male and female*
> *created he them. And God blessed them, and God said*
> *unto them, Be fruitful, and multiply, and replenish*
> *the earth, and subdue it: and have dominion over*
> *the fish of the sea, and over the fowl of the air, and*
> *over every living thing that moveth upon the earth.*
> Genesis 1:27-28 (KJV)

We are created to function together, to distinctively pro-create together, to be united in peace and harmony, and to manage other creatures with the dominion God gave us to do so. These human responsibilities and roles must never be manipulated and undermined by some worldly human selfish agenda.

The real deal about gender equality isn't to fit a few women into key positions or to favour fewer professional women. Neither should it be used as an avenue for people to pick offence, fight, or quarrel over every slightest opportunity. Rather it is an organised system for a better society. Rationally, gender equality exists for all humans to live together, attain their goals, and advance to success together. Thus, Christians, Muslims, all religious orders, and politicians and people in authority should not allow issues surrounding sexism to damage society norms and values.

During International Women's Day in 2017, UK stats released showed that 71% of women now pass their GCSE Leaving Certifications compared to 61% for men. In third-level education, 37% female now further their education compared to 27% of men. In Parliament, 30% are female, and in business, 35% are female CEOs.

These stats are commendable, some women emphasised that they should not be forced into competition with men. These mid-thirties women still wanted to marry and have a family. Some women also felt that while gender equality is promoted and encouraged, men should not be undermined, consciously or unconsciously attacked psychologically or mentally, or deliberately victimized in achieving the liberation for women. Many women agree that the role of man in headship should be protected, and a woman's ability to help and multitask should be maintained.

Nevertheless, in the Lord woman is not independent of man, nor is man independent of woman. For as woman came from man, so also man is born of woman. But everything comes from God.
1 Corinthians 11:11-12 (NIV)

SEXUALLY EXPLICIT

God has strong mandates concerning sexual conduct. From the beginning, one man and one woman until death has been the formula for success. God invented sex, love and companionship so that man would not be alone, and children would be nurtured and brought up in loving families to become responsible adults. Relationships were designed to be based on mutual love, respect and affection shared by both genders. God wants us to love and cherish, in sickness and in health, for better or worse. Marriage was created for the long haul, not as a fair-weather relationship subject to dissolution or divorce for any infraction. God commanded Noah and his family to go forth and be fruitful and multiply to repopulate the earth. Our loving God gave sex as a good gift for married couples. There is nothing lewd, crude, or undesirable about it.

> *Marriage should be honoured by all, and the marriage bed kept pure, for God will judge the adulterer and all the sexually immoral.*
> Hebrews 13:4 (NIV)

> *Let him kiss me with the kisses of his mouth: for thy love is better than wine.*
> Song of Solomon 1:2 (KJV)

The world has different ideas about sex, marriage and morality. Our norms of what is acceptable have become irrationally tolerant of deviance from God's plan. People around the globe are practicing anything and everything they deem desirable, and it presents a huge challenge and obstacle to decency. This is not new, but it is increasing and pervasive.

> *It is actually reported that there is sexual immorality among you, and of a kind that even pagans do not tolerate: A man is sleeping with his father's wife.*
> 1 Corinthians 5:1 (NIV)

Moral standards are taking a dip and sexual immorality is increasing. Christian values are being undermined, neglected, unmentioned and even sometimes threatened or regarded as obsolete. Even Christians who sit in places of policy making and are influential in the law and governance cannot speak up to be heard.

Lots of people are now inclined to sexual experiments, some obsessed with fantasies and orgies. Although immoral, these proclivities are discussed in the press and in parliament under the guise of freedom of expression and choice, fuelling separation and divorce. Lustful pleasure and promiscuity are contradictory to the pursue of godliness required of Christians. Sexual explicitness has become the selling point for most music, fashion, movie and drama concepts. It has become the sugar-coated flavour for deviation from God's plan.

Watch out! The momentum is in the rise, do not be caught.

> *The acts of the flesh are obvious: sexual immorality, impurity and debauchery; idolatry and witchcraft; hatred, discord, jealousy, fits of rage, selfish ambition, dissensions, factions and envy; drunkenness, orgies, and the like. I warn you, as I did before, that those who live like this will not inherit the kingdom of God.*
> Galatians 5:19-21 (NIV)

Why there are no discussions about the benefits of heterosexuality, abstinence from sex before marriage and remaining faithful in relationships? Because we do not have these conversations, depravity continues, as does diseases, sickness, and unnatural affection.

Christians are not rising up to discuss the immense benefits and blessings available to those who are faithful in their relationships. Isn't faithfulness a good recipe that encourages genuine love, earns trust and nurtures bonding? The fruit of the Spirit include love, joy, peace, patience, kindness, goodness, faithfulness, gentleness, and self-control, all beneficial to those who practice it. Couples in Christ should embrace these traits.

The undermining of Christian values continues to hinder most youngsters and the general population from leading quality relationships. Many have robbed themselves of peace, joy, and love in the Lord and for one another. The solution isn't far-fetched: Repent and confess Jesus as Lord and Saviour.

When a man or woman intends to separate from his or her spouse, the man wants to be free while the woman wants to be lose. They want to eliminate accountability to their partners, and have the freedom to engage in newfound sexual interests, which motivates them to leave home.

I knew a woman who made a bogus accusation to the police. She accused her husband of tearing her dress and therefore considered her husband abusive. She eventually frustrated her husband out of the house because she wanted the opportunity to meet with another man. One day I saw her with this other man. She tried to introduce him to me as her new husband. However, what goes around comes around. After couple of months, the new man abandoned her in favor of his actual wife and their bonds of matrimony.

> *Ye adulterers and adulteresses, know ye not that the friendship of the world is enmity with God? whosoever therefore will be a friend of the world is the enemy of God.*
> James 4:4 (KJV)

CHAPTER 3

GOD'S MANUAL FOR SUCCESSFUL FAMILY RELATIONSHIPS

The joining of a man and woman in marriage started way back with Adam and Eve. The God of all creation brought both together by divine purpose. And the man Adam said, 'This is now bone of my bones and flesh of my flesh' (Genesis 2:23). This explains why at some stage in life, a man leaves his father and his mother and is united unto his wife. Therefore, the two of them become one in marriage.

Once they are joined together in one accord, they are no longer strangers or aliens to one another, but family. Everything they do is done in unity and with mutual purpose. They share their wealth and bodies with one another without fear or shame.

It is better to marry than to burn with passion. God's design is for each man to have his own wife, and each woman to have her own husband. The husband should fulfil his marital duties to his wife, and likewise the wife to her husband. The wife's body does not belong to her alone but also to her husband. In the same way, the husband's body does not belong to him alone, but also to his wife.

> *Do not deprive each other except perhaps by mutual consent and for a time, so that you may devote yourselves to prayer. Then come together again so that Satan will not tempt you because of your lack of self-control.*
> 1 Corinthians 7:5 (NIV)

Enjoy life with your wife or husband whom you are commanded to love all the days of your life. Time slips away and all the time you toil and struggle for success, riches and fame will be fleeting and meaningless if you don't enjoy the love of your family as God intended.

> *What do people gain from all their labours at which they toil under the sun?*
> Ecclesiastes 1:3 (NIV)

> *He who finds a wife finds what is good and receives favour from the Lord.*
> Proverbs 18:22 (NIV)

> *But from the beginning of the creation God made them male and female. For this cause shall a man leave his father and mother, and cleave to his wife; And they twain shall be one flesh: so then they are no more twain, but one flesh. What therefore God hath joined together, let not man put asunder.*
> Mark 10:6-9 (KJV)

God created marriage based on the principle of submission. Both husband and wife must submit to each other to their role in godly fashion. God didn't make one gender superior and the other inferior. They are equal, and both have roles to fulfil to sustain a happy marriage. There is no intended gender superiority or inferiority in fulfilling each other's designated commitment for the marriage to be sustained.

The Bible has many Scriptures that outline what God has in mind for a happy marriage.

> *Submit to one another out of reverence for Christ.*
> Ephesians 5:21 (NIV)

Submission is mutual, done out of love and for the sake of peace and harmony, not out of fear or for monetary advantage or material comfort. God knew that when two people submit themselves to each other, a partnership would develop filled with love. God ordained submission.

> *Wives, submit yourselves to your own husbands as you do to the Lord. For the husband is the head of the wife as Christ is the head of the church, his body, of which he is the Saviour. Now as the church submits to Christ, so also wives should submit to their husbands in everything.*
> Ephesians 5:22-24 (NIV)

In the worldly regime, *submission* is a dirty word. Society tells us that women are independent and do not have to submit to anyone, least of all men. But God knew that there must be a head of the household, and he chose the man to be that head. What that means is when a woman is submissive (which does not mean being a doormat), she is under God's protection for being obedient and the man is responsible to God for the headship of his household.

Submission is not a one-way street. God had more to say about it.

> *Husbands, love your wives, just as Christ loved the church and gave himself up for her to make her holy, cleansing her by the washing with water through the word, and to present her to himself as a radiant church, without stain or wrinkle or any other blemish, but*

> *holy and blameless. In this same way, husbands ought to love their wives as their own bodies. He who loves his wife loves himself. After all, no one ever hated their own body, but they feed and care for their body, just as Christ does the church—for we are members of his body. "For this reason a man will leave his father and mother and be united to his wife, and the two will become one flesh." This is a profound mystery—but I am talking about Christ and the church. However, each one of you also must love his wife as he loves himself, and the wife must respect her husband.*
> Ephesians 5:25-33 (NIV)

What does it mean? Wife: Submit to and respect your man. Husband: Love, pamper, and treat your wife with sacrificial love so that she will be happy, and life will be pleasant for you. God intended for a man and woman to marry and to stop being two separate people. Marriage creates a spiritual union of one flesh. They have to depend on God's grace and keep their sense of humour sometimes to get along, but if they follow God's plan, they will have a happy and full life together, a partnership for life.

In marriage, you don't stagnate. You keep learning, keep loving, and keep following Christ. Couples that study God's Word, pray together, bring up their children in the fear and admonition of the Lord, tithe, do all things as unto Christ, and submit to each other will love life and have much joy that the world doesn't understand because the world doesn't have it. Christians who cultivate soft approaches turn away wrath and avoid grievous word that disturb the household peace. Those who also learn to respect, reverence and appreciate each other will have joy and peace even in hard times.

> *A gentle answer turns away wrath,*
> *but a harsh word stirs up anger.*
> Proverbs 15:1 (NIV)

A couple has a rule that makes a great deal of sense to harmony. The rule is simple and goes like this: It is okay to get mad but only one of us can be mad at the same time. The other must listen quietly and calmly until the mad partner is finished venting.

Following this practice can be challenging at first, but once you learn to swallow your pride and get the hang of it, it becomes habit and is comfortable and easy to do. The Holy Spirit will help you navigate disagreements and comfort you. Remember: You can do all things through Christ who strengthens you (Philippians 4:13).

Marriage is not a bed of roses; but many couples enter the institution with rose coloured glasses. They have images and expectations of marriage reminiscent of a free ticket to Disneyland or offer for a free lunch. Don't expect your partner to make you feel complete and whole, or to make you happy. If you are not happy with yourself, how can someone else make you happy? Marriage is hard work and if you are not ready to commit to the work, you are not ready to get married.

Both partners may have some unspoken expectations of marriage that are not realistic. Often, they stem from past experience or fantasy. If any of these thoughts sound familiar, you might want to reconsider getting married.

- When I get married, we will live happily ever after and have no problems.
- I will be pampered all the time.
- The husband pays for everything.
- The wife cooks and cleans and does all the housework.

Lots of people dive into marriage with amazing thoughts, though unrealistic expectations. Unfortunately, they sometimes exit as quickly as they entered, because the terms and conditions were not what they anticipated.

The divorce rate is growing and little seems to stop it. Wonder what would happen if preachers, imams, elders, parents and marriage counsellors invested more effort to ensure that young couples understand the rigors and stumbling blocks of marriage? What if couples were taught to fight fair, compromise, and listen to their spouses? I suspect the divorce and separation rate would decline.

IMPLICATIONS OF INFIDELITY

God gives one justifiable reason for divorce, and that is infidelity.

> *And I say unto you, Whosoever shall put away his wife, except it be for fornication, and shall marry another, committeth adultery: and whoso marrieth her which is put away doth commit adultery.*
> Matthew 19:9 (KJV)

Being unfaithful breaks the marriage vows, the partner's heart, and hinders love, trust and unity. It can destroy the relationship. I have never counselled a couple dealing with the aftermath of adultery who did wish it had never happened (both husband and wife). But you cannot undo what is done, so you must ask the Holy Spirit to give you wisdom and to warn you to avoid temptation long before it becomes adultery.

Although not adultery, another large hurdle in a marriage is when a man fails to provide for his household. Being lazy or wasteful or unconcerned with family welfare is a form of broken trust with treacherous ramifications.

> *But if any provide not for his own, and specially for those of his own house, he hath denied the faith, and is worse than an infidel.*
> 1 Timothy 5:8 (KJV)

GENDER RESPECT IN MARRIAGE

Women need love and men need respect. Did you know the Bible mandates husbands to lavish affection and shower their wives with love? The Word says he must love his wife as he loves himself. Likewise, women must respect their husbands.

> *Husbands, in the same way be considerate as you live with your wives, and treat them with respect as the weaker partner and as heirs with you of the gracious gift of life, so that nothing will hinder your prayers.*
> 1 Peter 3:7 (NIV)

The Bible provides a steadfast unchanging glimpse of what marriage can be. Fundamental gender roles are stipulated, so when couples are ready to get into marriage, they already know what is expected of them and how to conduct themselves so that they can handle challenges when they arise. When they don't know what to do, they can open the Word and let God speak to their situation.

> *All scripture is given by inspiration of God, and is profitable for doctrine, for reproof, for correction, for instruction in righteousness:*
> 2 Timothy 3:16 (KJV)

CHRISTIAN MARRIAGE IN THE COMMUNITY

The Word of God is the true foundation of marriage, not our individual worldly choices. The Bible says not be unequally yoked (2 Corinthians 6:14), but sometimes a believer is married to an unbeliever, or in a marriage of two unbelievers, one gets saved. Scripture says it is okay to stay together in that case as long as the unbeliever is content to dwell with the believer.

Through the believer's quiet spirit and exemplary lifestyle for the unbeliever to observe daily, it is possible that the unbeliever will be saved as a result. The believing partner creates an open invitation for the unbeliever to be converted. It is hard to resist God when you see your partner transformed by the Word. You want what they have so the leap is easier. This situation creates an evangelism window, where either the man or the woman who is Christian has the opportunity to win over the spouse to God's Kingdom by demonstrating good character in love, humbleness, kindness, peace, and patience.

> *To the rest I say this (I, not the Lord): If any brother has a wife who is not a believer and she is willing to live with him, he must not divorce her. And if a woman has a husband who is not a believer and he is willing to live with her, she must not divorce him. For the unbelieving husband has been sanctified through his wife, and the unbelieving wife has been sanctified through her believing husband. Otherwise your children would be unclean, but as it is, they are holy. But if the unbeliever leaves, let it be so. The brother or the sister is not bound in such circumstances; God has called us to live in peace.*
> 1 Corinthians 7:12-15 (NIV)

The world watches how Christians interact in marriage and compare what they see to what nonbeliever do. Live such good Christian lives among unbelievers or pagans that they will want what you have.

> *let your light shine before others, that they may see your good deeds and glorify your Father in heaven.*
> Matthew 5:16 (NIV)

Worldly people are still amazed to see Christian couples who love and respect each other. They may wonder how you get along so well, where the self-control and patience come from, and why you are not out partying with the rest of the world. They may never tell you, but they will want to know what your secret is. To have such happiness may seem impossible to them, but we know that all things are possible through Christ. If given the chance, tell them about your wonderful Jesus.

The worldly regime does not understand the context of submission in Christian marriage. To most, submission means subordinate. But in a Bible-based marriage, submission occurs in both directions and is meant to honour the spouse. When witnessed in action, the ability to submit in marriage without resentment is an exemplary model to behold. The very act of submission brings honour to marriage, the marriage partners, and to God who created marriage. It can also potentially convert people in community to faith in Christ by the grace of God and your example and testimony.

Submissive wives are sexy women. Husbands crave respect, and when wives give it to them through submission, they win their husbands not by beauty or fine clothes, but by behaviour, character and purity. Respectful submission from wives make it easy for husbands to carry out God's directive to show unfailing love and respect to their wives as the weaker vessel. Husbands will want to nurture their wives and live in harmony. The Bible says that if husbands don't, their prayers are hindered. Submission must be pretty important if it affects prayers.

The husband also should always remember to show unfailing love and respect, knowing the wives are weaker vessel. To humbly nurture them and live in harmony, so the husband prayers may not be hindered.

> *Wives, in the same way submit yourselves to your own husbands so that, if any of them do not believe the word, they may be won over without words by the behavior of their wives, when they see the purity and reverence of your lives. Your beauty should not come from outward adornment, such as elaborate hairstyles and the wearing of gold jewelry or fine clothes. Rather, it should be that of your inner self, the unfading beauty of a gentle and quiet spirit, which is of great worth in God's sight. For this is the way the holy women of the past who put their hope in God used to adorn themselves. They submitted themselves to their own husbands, like Sarah, who obeyed Abraham and called him her lord. You are her daughters if you do what is right and do not give way to fear. Husbands, in the same way be considerate as you live with your wives, and treat them with respect as the weaker partner and as heirs with you of the gracious gift of life, so that nothing will hinder your prayers.*
> 1 Peter 3:1-7 (NIV)

Jesus wants us to be happy and experience love in the context of marriage in many ways: agape, sensual, family, and of course the love of God. As long as we follow the scriptural formula for marriage and family, we will be far less likely to fall prey to the vices of the worldly regime, and instead experience an abundance of peace, love, progress and will enjoy being together with our spouses and families.

Marriage made in heaven is possible if it is set on the solid foundation of God's Word. It does not fail. Marriage done God's way is forgiving, understanding, patient, obedient, bears fruti, and blossoms in fruitfulness.

If you keep my commands, you will remain in my love,
just as I have kept my Father's commands
and remain in his love.
John 15:10 (NIV)

HOW GOOD CHRISTIAN FAMILY RELATIONSHIPS CAN COMBAT YOUTH CRIME

Violent crime among our young people has spiralled out of control. Over the past five years the volume of crimes committed with knives has reached record highs. It is hard to remember a time when our cities had little violence and gang activity. Our streets are not safe anymore, and it creates pause to ponder how we got to this point.

Before many of those youths hit the streets to wreak havoc, they experienced havoc at home. They watched their parents and listened to their interactions. They saw, heard and experienced family life from an intimate perspective. The Bible tell us to

> *Train up a child in the way he should go:*
> *and when he is old, he will not depart from it.*
> Proverbs 22:6 (KJV)

Christian parents understand that Scripture to mean train children well, teach them strong moral values, help them navigate difficult choices, set good examples for them to emulate, and give them unconditional love. Reared in that kind of childhood environment, a young person has every opportunity to succeed and become a productive and respected adult.

But the opposite is also true. Just as you can train up a child for a good life, you can also (although perhaps inadvertently) train up a child for a troubled existence. If a child grows up in home where parents do not love each other, he learns that love is not important. If he grows up watching abuse, he learns that abusing those who cannot defend themselves is acceptable conduct. If he is the one being abused, he builds up anger inside because he is helpless to stop the abuse. That anger will eventually come out, perhaps in the form of criminal activity, bullying, suicidal or homicidal ideation, or any number of other negative responses brought on to combat the feelings of helplessness experienced as a child.

The long-term results of our actions as parents will be seen in our children decades down the road. If we work all the time and spend no time with our kids, we teach them that children are not important and that only making money to pay bills is worthwhile. That knowledge in a child's heart can lead to him or her growing up to be a workaholic or finding easier ways to make money (crime, drugs, etc.). If our kids witness strife, arguments, yelling, hateful words hurled in angry outbursts, infidelity, threats, or physical violence in the home, they learn and repeat those behaviours. The biggest bully in high school may be the one who is bullied most at home. The boy who is always looking for a fight may be the one who sees fights at home regularly. The girl with an absent father who watches her mother out with numerous men regularly follows in her mum's footsteps when she begins dating. Children who see their parents abusing alcohol and drugs often grow up with substance abuse problems.

Let's face it: Taking care of your children is your job. What you do now is the foundation for the rest of your children's lives. When you don't care for them, they suffer. This suffering manifests itself in uncertainty, curiosity, strange feelings, anxiety, anger, loneliness, fear, frustration, feeling invisible, longing for love, and loss of identity. In addition, children tend to blame themselves for your problems. They live in small worlds that revolve around themselves and they have not yet acquired the mental abilities to reason that your issues are not their fault. If you ask a five-year-old why Daddy is gone, you might be surprised at the answer. Children blame themselves when things go wrong with parents. They attribute the reason a parent is absent to something they did or didn't do, and they carry that guilt. Then they watch the remaining parent try to do the work of both parents, sometimes working long hours to provide, and the loneliness deepens. Young people need human contact and understanding, they need to socialize, and they need to belong. If the parents are absent or always working, they look elsewhere to fill the emotional void. If they make poor choices, they often encounter negative peer pressure to do things they know they shouldn't do.

> *Do not be misled: "Bad company*
> *corrupts good character."*
> 1 Corinthians 15:33 (NIV)

Build a good foundation for your children. There are kids who grow up in adversity who later succeed against all odds, but those are few and far between.

> *If the foundations be destroyed,*
> *what can the righteous do?*
> Psalm 11:3 (KJV)

Although there is no scientific correlation or proven cause and effect relationship established by research, remember when the divorce rate was low? So was the youth crime rate! Now that the divorce rate is high, so is the youth crime rate. I theorize that supply and demand are at work. The demand for two-parent loving families is high, but the supply is low, so the price we pay goes up. Part of that price is increased crime and delinquency among our young people.

How do we as Christians play our part to help fix broken families and lives? We can start by setting good examples for unbelievers to follow. Then we can encourage couples to solve their issues amicably instead with of divorce or separation. When divorce seems eminent, we might suggest that parents keep their kids out of their fights by not spewing hatred for each other that could turn children's hearts away.

> *A good man out of the good treasure of his heart*
> *brings forth good; and an evil man out of the evil*

> *treasure of his heart brings forth evil. For out of*
> *the abundance of the heart his mouth speaks.*
> Luke 6:45 (KJV)

> *But those things which proceed out of the mouth come*
> *forth from the heart; and they defile the man.*
> *For out of the heart proceed evil thoughts, murders,*
> *adulteries, fornications, thefts, false witness, blasphemies:*
> Matthew 15:18-19 (KJV)

When parents are in the middle of emotional pain, they sometimes forget that once children enter their lives, it was no longer what is best for "Me! Me! Me!" The focus must shift to what is best for "Them! Them! Them!" When God blesses a family with children, He also places responsibility for their wellbeing with the parents.

> *Lo, children are an heritage of the Lord:*
> *and the fruit of the womb is his reward.*
> Psalm 127:3 (KJV)

In your Christian home, you can protect your children from the worldly regime outside your door by exercising strict management and setting hard and fast rules that do not change. Give your children consistent expectations, reward them for meeting or exceeding those expectations, and follow through with appropriate consequences when they do not. By doing so, you will develop good moral character in your children. They will not always appreciate your efforts, especially when you don't let them go to that house party, or spend the night with that friend, or allow that other friend to visit in your home because they are a bad influence. They may initially resent you getting involved in their choice of friends, sports, games and other activities, but will later be glad you were engaged with their lives and cared enough to participate in their decisions.

RECOMMENDATION FOR YOUTHS

Christian parent, you have the capacity to effectuate powerful intervention against youth delinquency for your children. How? Find wholesome activities for your children to be involved in. It is easy, but it takes a little time to explore your options. Where do you look? Church, school, and the community.

In the church, you can find youth groups that provide social activities to keep kids off the street and focused on godly pursuits. Many churches have Sunday school, Bible studies, youth groups and events, and children's choirs. Going to church for more than sermons gives productive outlet for a child's energy, enthusiasm, social needs, spiritual growth, and use of time.

In the school, look for extra-curricular activities such as clubs, events, tutoring opportunities, sports, and academic competitions.

In the community, look for sports, hobbies and crafts, dance, drama, and other ways to occupy spare time while gaining skills that can be continued into adulthood.

When you promote physical, mental, emotional, social, and spiritual well-being by giving your children things to do that are engaging, fun, and rewarding, you leave little time for them to get involved with unsupervised groups. Left to their own use of time, youth affiliations can deteriorate into gang and criminal activities, fights, drug and alcohol abuse, teenage pregnancy, school dropouts, disrespect to adults including parents and teachers, and involvement with the law enforcement.

REAL LIFE TESTIMONIES

A young man about twenty-one years old once told me that when his mother wanted marijuana, he got it for her and smoked it with her. It took a bit for me to wrap my mind around that unhealthy image of a mother-son relationship. He told me he often funded her expenses and habits.

You guessed it – yes, I told him to cease feeding his mother's drug habit and stop the unwholesome co-dependence of their relationship. A mother's job is to guide her son, to chasten him for wrongdoing, to lead him in paths of righteousness. Yet, this mother mortgaged her right and authority over her son because of a drug habit and poor choices. How can she exercise her God-given authority if she depends on him for her drugs?

In 2017, a female judge in Finland stated that women who are intoxicated in public places are increasing their chances of being raped. A feminist organisation in the United Kingdom launched an attack against the judge by condemning her advice. The judge had no intention to provoke any group or gender, but simply wanted to reduce the vulnerability of women becoming victims of sexual assault. A Finnish victim of those circumstances the judge warned against stepped forward to endorse the judge's position and swayed the opposition.

Christian parents need to stand their ground with their children in the face of chaos such as sexual assault and diminishing moral and ethical standard. The worldly regime makes false proclamations about modern society that would be easy for youths to absorb, so we must ground our children in God's Word and guide their steps.

QUALITIES OF GOOD FATHERS (ELDERS):

- Must be blameless
- Husband of one wife
- Faithful to wife and family
- His children are trained to believe and are not wild and disobedient.
- A good manager of God's household
- Self – controlled
- Not quick tempered
- Not given to drunkenness
- Not violent
- Not pursuing dishonest gain
- Must be hospitable
- One who loves what is good
- Upright person
- Holy and disciplined
- Trustworthy both with information and message of Christian doctrine
- Not a deceiver or hypocrite
- Sound in faith, in love and in endurance

QUALITIES OF GOOD MOTHERS:

- Demonstrates holy behaviour
- Not false accusers
- Not given to much wine
- Able to teach what is good
- Willing to teach younger women to love their husband and children
- Self-controlled and pure
- To be busy at home
- To be kind
- To be subject to their husbands
- Obedient that the Word of God be not blasphemed
- Not slanderers
- Noble character and productivity
- Builder and keeper of the home

QUALITIES OF PARENTAL ADVICE TO THEIR CHILDREN:

- Parents should set good examples by doing what is good
- Teach them to be self-controlled and pure
- Show integrity, seriousness, and soundness of speech in their deeds, so those who intend to oppose may have nothing bad to say
- Show the younger ones patterns of good work and sincerity
- Teach them the need to obey their parents in the Lord, and to honour their fathers and mothers
- Bring them up in the nurture and admonition of the Lord, not provoking them to wrath
- Teach the children not to be deceived or disobedient nor be given to or enslaved by all kinds of passions and pleasures
- Encourage them to stay on the part of the just so they can shine

As parents, we must do all we can to advocate for good lifestyle choices and demonstrate kindness, good character, genuine love, trust, peace, faith in God and love for one another. The worldly regime exerts pressure through most social circles of influence, but we as believers must not allow ourselves to be swayed or caught up in prevailing webs of impatience, hate, selfishness or sinful desires that revel against the body and spirit. Our legacies are lived out through our progeny, so we must place great weight on values and high standards and be careful what we do because our children are watching and learning and copying our examples.

*This I say then, Walk in the Spirit,
and ye shall not fulfil the lust of the flesh.*
Galatians 5:16 (KJV)

SHOW ATTITUDE FOR GRATITUDE

Reverend Harvey 'Onelove' Simpson, Chaplain at Big Spring, Texas, expressed the need to show a good attitude for gratitude. He lives by these principles:

- Never take anyone for granted. Instead, show respect and courtesy.
- Don't miss an opportunity to appreciate one another.
- Be genuine with the people you come across every day.

Honour all men. Love the brotherhood.
Fear God. Honour the king.
1 Peter 2:17 (KJV)

CHAPTER 4

WHEN A MAN LOVES A WOMAN

God really loved Adam. He created this man, fellowshipped with him, let him name all the animals, and paid close enough attention that He realized that even though all other animals had partners, Adam was alone. God knew that was not good.

> *And the LORD God said, It is not good that the man should be alone; I will make him an help meet for him.*
> Genesis 2:18 (KJV)

God knows how to fix every problem, so He decided to give Adam a partner in life. He made all the animals male and female, so He chose to create a female for Adam, too.

> *So the Lord God caused the man to fall into a deep sleep; and while he was sleeping, he took one of the man's ribs and then closed up the place with flesh. Then the Lord God made a woman from the rib he had taken out of the man, and he brought her to the man.*
> Genesis 2:21 (NIV)

As expected, Adam was pleased with this woman God gave him.

The man said,

"This is now bone of my bones and flesh of my flesh; she shall be called 'woman,' for she was taken out of man."
Genesis 2:22 (NIV)

Adam and his wife were both naked, and they felt no shame.
Genesis 2:25 (NIV)

From the beginning, man and woman have been suitable companions for each other, with capacity to form inseparable bonds. God made man the head of the home, and woman his help meet. God put them both in charge of children and intended for them to work together for the good of the family and to multiply and populate the earth. God knew that potential of man and woman partnering in life and the happiness that could be claimed by working in harmony. When the two follow scriptural principles, they can benefit their community and church, establish prosperous businesses, and be a blessing to their city and nation.

I speak this wisdom gleaned from personal experience. I am one of seven children in my family (six boys, one girl). My parents stayed together through thick and thin, and they agreed to agree, and sometimes they agreed to disagree. They forged and maintained an amazing partnership that has lasted over 50 years. They celebrated their golden anniversary in December 2015.

My mother, an enthusiastic homemaker, has spent her life looking after the home, my dad, and her children. In similar fashion, my dad, the breadwinner, worked hard to provide for the family. They were always a team, sharing ideas and making decisions for the common good. They had no selfish motives. They have always accommodated, advised, compromised, and understood each other's needs. They never separated, were never vindictive, and supported each other in every way possible (materially, financially, physically, and emotionally).

My parents have been the best role models I could have asked for. They are the epitome of lasting companionship in marriage and I give God the glory for their longevity and togetherness. Though I remember few incidents and challenging times during adolescence, my clear observation was that those times never lasted. My parents defied all odds and stuck together like glue with mutual commitment.

God put some rules in place to ensure success in marriage.

- Keep your relatives out of your business.

Therefore shall a man leave his father and his mother, and shall cleave unto his wife: and they shall be one flesh.
Genesis 2:24 (KJV)

- Love your wife. God gave her to you to love, not to mistreat or ignore. That love will take many forms over a lifetime together: emotional, agape, sensual, and spiritual. If you shower a woman with love, it pleases God's heart, gives you favour and your prayers are not hindered.

Husbands, love your wives, even as Christ also loved the church, and gave himself for it;
Ephesians 5:25 (KJV)

- Love each other. Love is a witness to devotion that bridges every gap that could hamper a relationship. That devotion means being dedicated to walking and working with team spirit.

Love is patient, love is kind. It does not envy, it does not boast, it is not proud. It does not dishonour

> *others, it is not self-seeking, it is not easily angered,*
> *it keeps no record of wrongs. Love does not delight*
> *in evil but rejoices with the truth. It always protects,*
> *always trusts, always hopes, always perseveres.*
> 1 Corinthians 13:4-7 (NIV)

> *And now these three remain: faith, hope and love.*
> *But the greatest of these is love.*
> 1 Corinthians 13:13 (NIV)

- Dwell in harmony.

> *Can two walk together, except they be agreed?*
> Amos 3:3 (KJV)

> *Again I say unto you, That if two of you shall agree on*
> *earth as touching any thing that they shall ask, it shall*
> *be done for them of my Father which is in heaven.*
> Matthew 18:19 (KJV)

- Make your spouse a priority. It is easy to tell what is important to someone. They make it a priority. If a man loves his dog, he takes good care of it. If he loves his car, he keeps it in good running condition. If a woman loves her home, she keeps her apartment clean. Even more so, we must make our relationship a priority and care for it, keep it in good running condition, and keep it clean.

> *Above all, love each other deeply,*
> *because love covers over a multitude of sins.*
> 1 Peter 4:8 (NIV)

By now, you probably see the benefits of loving each other in marriage and walking together in teamwork, fellowship and compromise. It is good to enjoy your wife and make her happy. When she is happy, wellness in all its ramifications radiates from your union.

> *May your fountain be blessed, and may*
> *you rejoice in the wife of your youth.*
> Proverbs 5:18 (NIV)

The Bible speaks of a virtuous woman and the blessings of finding a good woman. All women have virtues and I implore you to seek out the virtues and good qualities in your wife.

> *Who can find a virtuous woman? for her price is far*
> *above rubies. The heart of her husband doth safely*
> *trust in her, so that he shall have no need of spoil. She*
> *will do him good and not evil all the days of her life.*
> Proverbs 31:10-12 (KJV)

> *Whoso findeth a wife findeth a good thing,*
> *and obtaineth favour of the Lord.*
> Proverbs 18:22 (KJV)

Both man and woman are necessary for propagation of the species. They do not exist independent of each other, so they might as well get along.

> *Nevertheless, in the Lord woman is not independent*
> *of man, nor is man independent of woman. For*
> *as woman came from man, so also man is born*
> *of woman. But everything comes from God.*
> 1 Corinthians 11:11-12 (NIV)

God commands us to dwell in unity and treat wives with love and respect, remembering they are the weaker sex, but still heirs in Christ.

> *Likewise, ye husbands, dwell with them according to knowledge, giving honour unto the wife, as unto the weaker vessel, and as being heirs together of the grace of life; that your prayers be not hindered.*
> 1 Peter 3:7 (KJV)

> *Husbands, love your wives, and be not bitter against them.*
> Colossians 3:19 (KJV)

The responsibility to provide and care for one's household is the primary responsibility of a man, however, in situations where such is not possible there are considerations.

> *But if any provide not for his own, and specially for those of his own house, he hath denied the faith, and is worse than an infidel.*
> 1 Timothy 5:8 (KJV)

LESSONS LEARNED

Even today, I can recall the attention and care I received from my mother. She was first with get well wishes, tender hugs, and pats on the back when needed. She was just as kind to my siblings as she was to me.

Mom was divinely gifted with the ability to multi-task. In addition to being a wonderful homemaker, she also ran a chain of distributor and wholesale outlets in the confection industry and for production companies. She helped support our family and had a sense of self-sustainability. In my early teens, she invited me to work with her in sales and she taught me bargain strategies to work with Yoruba natives. From those early experiences, I developed entrepreneurial skills. Volunteering to work with her earned me incentives: clothing, cash allowances to use at boarding school, and enough funds to pay for snacks and other small items of interest to a teenager.

As I grew older, I went through a time of delinquency in which I got caught up in urban living leading to alcohol and drug abuse. My mother never stopped caring about me, but she urged me to get my act together and change my ways. Women instinctively know more than they verbalize. Because Mom's subtle ways of teaching and conveying advice were kind-hearted, peaceful and presented with natural affection, I was willing to change my ways; she inspired me to do better with her unconditional love.

> *The words of king Lemuel, the prophecy that his mother taught him. What, my son? and what, the son of my womb? and what, the son of my vows? Give not thy strength unto women, nor thy ways to that which destroyeth kings. It is not for kings, O Lemuel, it is not for kings to drink wine; nor for princes strong drink: Lest they drink, and forget the law, and pervert the judgment of any of the afflicted. Give strong drink*

> *unto him that is ready to perish, and wine unto those*
> *that be of heavy hearts. Let him drink, and forget*
> *his poverty, and remember his misery no more.*
> Proverbs 31:1-7 (KJV)

The Scripture tells us not to give our strength to harlots or a multitude of women, chasing after numerous women can be dangerous and afflicting.

> *My son, pay attention to my wisdom,*
> *turn your ear to my words of insight, that you may*
> *maintain discretion and your lips may preserve*
> *knowledge. For the lips of the adulterous woman drip*
> *honey, and her speech is smoother than oil; but in the end*
> *she is bitter as gall, sharp as a double-edged sword.*
> *Her feet go down to death; her steps lead straight to the*
> *grave. She gives no thought to the way of life;*
> *her paths wander aimlessly, but she does not know it.*
> Proverbs 5:1-6 (NIV)

With my mother's godly counsel, I did get my act together and received the correction she offered. In my adult life, her wisdom has helped me make good business decisions. When I was traveling in and out of Nigeria, she supervised and managed business on my behalf. She seems to have supernatural know-how and ability to make recommendations that are productive to my trade. All the wisdom and knowledge she willingly shares with me only makes love her more.

The Lord blessed me with a wonderful woman and wife, Esther, and four daughters and a son. They all have distinctive talents, character, and are blessed with God's grace.

> *Behold, I and the children whom the Lord hath
> given me are for signs and for wonders in Israel from
> the Lord of hosts, which dwelleth in mount Zion.*
> Isaiah 8:18 (KJV)

I am strengthened by God's grace, to nurture and maintain my treasured wife, daughters and son.

> *For where your treasure is, there will your heart be also.*
> Matthew 6:21 (KJV)

Our success as a family can be tied to Scripture:

> *However, each one of you also must love his wife as he
> loves himself, and the wife must respect her husband.*
> Ephesians 5:33 (NIV)

> *So ought men to love their wives as their own bodies.
> He that loveth his wife loveth himself.
> For no man ever yet hated his own flesh; but nourisheth
> and cherisheth it, even as the Lord the church:*
> Ephesians 5:28-29 (KJV)

In my youth, I had multiple affairs with women. My dad didn't like it and advised me that I must always take good care of the women I dated, being careful not to hurt them. My father had been a marvellous example of fatherhood, and a good husband, so I listened to his fatherly advice. He was right that there are far-reaching consequences for any man who is mean or abusive to a woman in his life. It is better to retain the woman's love than to create memories of hate.

THE EXPRESSION OF FAITH

There are many great matriarchs of the faith and through them, lives were changed, God's chosen people were saved, and rulers' hearts were swayed.

The Bible has numerous stories of women used of God to do His will and send His message:

- Mary, mother of Jesus. This virgin woman was blessed of all women to be the mother of Jesus. When the angel Gabriel told her that she would bear the son of God and call his name Jesus, she was receptive, didn't doubt it and was not afraid. Gabriel also entrusted her with information that her cousin Elizabeth would bear a son and his name would be John. Mary was able to rejoice with Elizabeth because God's messenger gave her the news.

> *And blessed is she that believed: for there shall be a performance of those things which were told her from the Lord.*
> Luke 1:45 (KJV)

- Abigail was married to a mean man, a wealthy Calebite (descendant of Caleb from the tribe of Judah) named Nabal. King David and his army protected Nabal's men when they were tending sheep nearby. King David's men were kind to Nabal's servants. When David was in Nabal's area, he sent his men to ask Nabal for some food for the troops. Nabal refused and insulted the king.

When word got back to David, he assembled three hundred men to go and kill every male Nabal owned.

When Abigail heard of her husband's wickedness and the King's plan, she loaded lots of food and wine on donkeys and went to find David before he killed her husband and all their male servants. She fell to her face before the king and used her woman's intuition to reach for the royalty in him. She explained that her husband was a fool (even his name meant fool) and wasn't worth having his blood on the king's hands. She explained David who had killed giants with a slingshot was noble and valiant and didn't need to waste his time on a loser like her husband. She appealed to his superior regal nature and asked him not to harm her husband. David was impressed and agreed to turn back.

Two weeks later, Nabal died. David sent for Abigail to be his wife. She buried a fool and married a king because she exercised wisdom.

> *For wisdom is a defence, and money is a defence:*
> *but the excellency of knowledge is,*
> *that wisdom giveth life to them that have it.*
> Ecclesiastes 7:12 (KJV)

Nabal was lucky that Abigail was willing to prostrate herself and apologize to King David on behalf of her husband. When a man is mean, a woman is not eager to negotiate or intercede or negotiate favour for him. A woman can be subtle, calm, meek, and willing to use the right set of words and polite approaches to win her battles. Her gentleness and soft words can soften a man's anger and dissipate his wrath.

> *A gentle answer turns away wrath,*
> *but a harsh word stirs up anger.*
> Proverbs 15:1 (NIV)

- Joanna, wife of Chuza who managed King Herod Antipas' household, was healed of evil spirits by Jesus. She became a loyal follower and supported Jesus and His disciples. After Jesus death on Calvary, the Gospel of Luke tells us that she was one of the three women (the other two were Mary Magdelene and Jesus' mother Mary) who came to the garden tomb bringing spices for the burial.

> *It was Mary Magdalene, Joanna, Mary the mother* of James, *and the other women* with them, who told these things to the apostles.
> Luke 24:10 (KJV)

- The Samaritan woman at the well met Jesus and he was able to share his message with the Samaritan community through her.

> *Then, leaving her water jar, the woman went back to the town and said to the people, "Come, see a man who told me everything I ever did. Could this be the Messiah?" They came out of the town and made their way toward him.*
> John 4:28-30 (NIV)

- Pilate's wife intervened on behalf of Jesus when her husband the governor adjudicated Jesus' case. God gave her a dream about Jesus and she sent a message swiftly to her husband telling him to have nothing to do with harming Jesus. Pilate got the message and said that he had found no fault in this man and washed his hands of the matter. Pilot's actions didn't save Jesus from being crucified, but they did exemplify the power of a woman's intuition and inner knowing.

> *When he was set down on the judgment seat, his wife sent unto him, saying, Have thou nothing to do with that just man: for I have suffered many things this day in a dream because of him.*
> Matthew 27:19 (KJV)

- Esther was a Jewish woman selected to replace Queen Vashti in King Ahaseurus (also known in Greek as Xerxes). Among the king's influential men was an evil man named Haman. He hated the Jewish people and especially Esther's Uncle Mordecai because he wouldn't stoop and bow to Haman.

Haman conspired to have all Jews killed on a certain day. Mordecai got word to the queen of the edict. Esther called for a fast and then did something that could have led to her death. She approached King Ahaseurus without an invitation. The king had a choice to extend his sceptre to her so she was welcome to enter, or have her killed for boldly coming to his throne without permission. Xerxes extended his sceptre and the queen used her woman's intuition to make her petition known to the king.

Esther invited the king and Haman to a feast for three days in a row. Each day the king offered her up to half his kingdom. All she had to do was tell him what she wanted.

On the third day, she revealed Haman's plan and her Jewish heritage. Xerxes was outraged and hanged Haman and all his sons on gallows intended for Jews. The says that Esther was there *for such as this*. Her willingness to risk her life resulted in her saving her people.

For if thou altogether holdest thy peace at this time, then shall there enlargement and deliverance arise to the Jews from another place; but thou and thy father's house shall be destroyed: and who knoweth whether thou art come to the kingdom for such a time as this?
Esther 4:14 (KJV)

A caring woman will do whatever it takes to find solutions for her household and compatible spouse. Therefore, it is wise for a man to constantly show love to his woman, knowing that she will most certainly reciprocate even at tough and challenging times.

And let us not be weary in well doing: for in due season we shall reap, if we faint not.
Galatians 6:9 (KJV)

BLESSED MOTHER TERESA'S PRAYER

People are often unreasonable,
Irrational, and self-centred.
Forgive them anyway.
If you are kind, people may accuse
You of selfish, ulterior motives.
Be kind anyway.
If you are successful, you will win
some unfaithful friends and some
genuine enemies. Succeed anyway.
If you are honest and sincere
People may deceive you. Be honest
And sincere anyway. What you
Spend years creating, others
Could destroy overnight.
Create anyway. If you find serenity
And happiness, some may
Be jealous. Be happy anyway.
The good you do today, will often
Be forgotten. Do good anyway.
Give the best you have, and it will
Never be enough.
Give your best anyway.
In the final analysis, it is between
You and God. It was never
Between you and them anyway.
Blessed Mother Teresa

SCRIPTURE QUOTATIONS

SCRIPTURE QUOTATIONS

*Come now, and let us reason together,
saith the Lord: though your sins be as scarlet, t
hey shall be as white as snow; though they be
red like crimson, they shall be as wool.
If ye be willing and obedient, ye shall
eat the good of the land:*
Isaiah 1:18-19 (KJV)

Think not that I am come to destroy the law, or the prophets: I am not come to destroy, but to fulfil.
Matthew 5:17 (KJV)

SCRIPTURE QUOTATIONS

If ye love me, keep my commandments.
John 14:15 (KJV)

He that saith, I know him, and keepeth not his commandments, is a liar, and the truth is not in him. But whoso keepeth his word, in him verily is the love of God perfected: hereby know we that we are in him.
1 John 2:4-5 (KJV)

SCRIPTURE QUOTATIONS

Not every one that saith unto me, Lord, Lord, shall enter into the kingdom of heaven; but he that doeth the will of my Father which is in heaven.
Matthew 7:21 (KJV)

But he said, Yea rather, blessed are they that hear the word of God, and keep it.
Luke 11:28 (KJV)

SCRIPTURE QUOTATIONS

If a man say, I love God, and hateth his brother, he is a liar: for he that loveth not his brother whom he hath seen, how can he love God whom he hath not seen?
1 John 4:20 (KJV)

This is a faithful saying, and worthy of all acceptation, that Christ Jesus came into the world to save sinners; of whom I am chief.
1 Timothy 1:15 (KJV)

NOTES

NOTES

NOTES

NOTES

NOTES

NOTES

NOTES

Note from the Publisher

Are you a first time author?

Not sure how to proceed to get your book published?
Want to keep all your rights and all your royalties?
Want it to look as good as a Top 10 publisher?
Need help with editing, layout, cover design?
Want it out there selling in 90 days or less?

Visit our website for some exciting new options!

www.chalfant-eckert-publishing.com

Made in the USA
Columbia, SC
14 November 2018